# ESOLVING POLITICAL DIFFERENCES

ited by Heather Kissock

Weigl

ALGARY

w.weigl.com

Published by Weigl Educational Publishers Limited
6325 10 Street SE
Calgary, Alberta, Canada
T2H 2Z9

Website: www.weigl.com

All of the Internet URLs given in the book were valid at the time of publication. However, due to the
dynamic nature of the Internet, some addresses may have changed, or sites may have ceased to exist
since publication. While the author and publisher regret any inconvenience this may cause readers,
no responsibility for any such changes can be accepted by either the author or the publisher.

Library and Archives Canada Cataloguing in Publication data available upon request.
Fax 403-233-7769 for the attention of the Publishing Records department.

ISBN 978-1-55388-933-5 (hard cover)
ISBN 978-1-55388-937-3 (soft cover)

Printed in the United States of America
1 2 3 4 5 6 7 8 9 0  13 12 11 10 09

Photograph Credits
Every reasonable effort has been made to trace ownership and to obtain
permission to reprint copyright material. The publishers would be pleased
to have any errors or omissions brought to their attention so that they may
be corrected in subsequent printings.

Weigl acknowledges Getty Images as its primary image supplier for this title.
Canadian Press: page 22.

Project Coordinators: Heather C. Hudak, Heather Kissock
Design: Terry Paulhus

We acknowledge the financial support of the Government of Canada through the Book Publishing
Industry Development Program (BPIDP) for our publishing activities.

# Contents

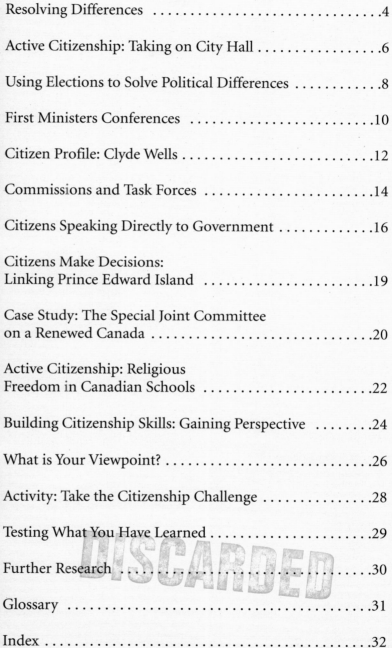

## Resolving Differences

People often have trouble making decisions because they cannot agree on the best way to do things. You have no doubt been in many situations where it was hard to act because people disagreed on what to do. What happens when a group of people want to go somewhere on a holiday but cannot agree on where they should go? How do you decide with you friends which movie you will see when everyone wants to see something differe

People often disagree on political issues, and it is true that these difference are sometimes very hard to resolve. Sometimes, people hold strong views

Couples often need to make decisions about where they will live and how they will spend money. Sometimes, they may have different ideas. They must work together to resolve their differences.

...ssues because the outcome can have ...rge impact on their lives. At each level ...overnment, there are issues that are ...d to resolve.

...zens in municipalities can have very ...erent views from one another on issues ...n as water quality, property taxes, ...ding codes, and other issues of local ...cern. At the provincial level, citizens ...e differing views about the use of ...ural resources, education issues, health ...welfare issues, and environmental ...cerns. There are also many issues at the ...ral level that citizens have different ...vs about.

...zens must be able to resolve their ...tical differences. When people can no ...er resolve their differences, they are ...able to make the decisions needed to ...o society running. An important part ...tizen participation is working to ...lve political differences so that the ...sion making can continue.

## ink About It

...w do you resolve differences of ...nion in order to make decisions ...home and at school?

People have different views of how to use Canada's natural resources, including forests.

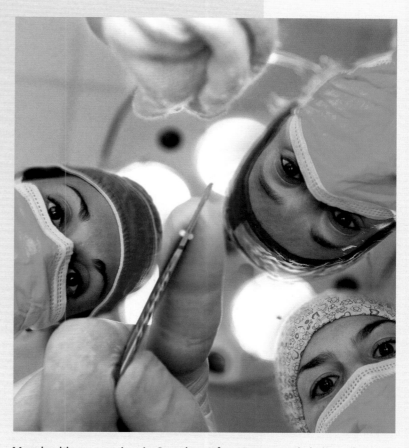

Most health care services in Canada are free. Some people believe there should be a fee.

# Active Citizenship: Taking on City Hall

There is a saying that states people cannot fight city hall. Whether it is true or not is up for debate. However, in 2008, a group of teenagers from Sarnia, Ontario proved that people can sometimes negotiate with city officials to get what they want.

While on their summer break, the teens used a remote part of a local park to build a BMX track. Much effort was put into the track's creation. The end result was an elaborate system of trails, ramps, and other obstacles.

BMX tracks are found in many cities and towns.

However, when the city discovered the track, its city council decided it had to demolished. The council had valid reas for making this decision. As the track w built on city property, the city could be held **liable** if anyone was hurt while us the track. Having a homemade bike pa on city property put the city in a tenuo legal position.

The boys did not want to see their har work bulldozed by the city. They came with a plan that they hoped would save their BMX park. They took this plan to both the media and city hall.

In it, they proposed that they post sign the track warning people that they use the facility at their own risk. This redu the city's liability if something went wrong. To improve the safety of the tra they also made a commitment to fill in dangerous holes, widen the ramps, and make corners easier to navigate.

The plan received much support from public. In one day, the mayor received almost 40 emails asking that the plan b implemented and the track be allowed stay. The local Kiwanis club even offere to help fund the improvements.

The mayor saw the plan's potential as He sent his staff down to the park to n with the boys and discuss the plan with them in detail. Following that meeting boys were given approval to implemen their plan. The BMX track was saved.

# ow to Negotiate With Government Officials

ty council members are elected to represent people living in specific areas. Part of their job is to listen to
izens to learn their wants and needs for the community. The entire council meets at regular times to discuss
portant matters. In many cases, the public is able to attend these meetings. People may make presentations to
e council on issues. The council may then vote in favour of or against the person's issue. These are some of the
ays you can bring an issue to the attention of a city council member in your area.

- research your topic and similar cases

- prepare a statement

- contact city officials to let them know your concerns

- meet with officials to present your case

- request a council vote on your case

- participate in a city hall meeting to share your
  statement with the public

## Think About It

What are some obstacles for citizens who want to
challenge government legislation? How can citizens
overcome these obstacles?

Prime Minister Brian Mulroney and U.S. President Ronald Reagan worked together to develop a trade agreement between Canada and the United States.

# Using Elections to Solve Political Differences

One of the most basic ways that citizens solve political differences is to hold elections. The main purpose of elections is to decide which candidates will best represent the citizens' interests and which group of candidates will form the government. Sometimes, however, elections focus on political issues more complex than choosing the correct candidate or party.

he past, elections have been held to
olve some issues. For example, the 1988
eral election focussed on the issue of
 **trade** with the United States. The
gressive Conservative government of
me Minister Brian Mulroney held talks
h the United States, and reached an
eement for a new trading deal with
er restrictions.

ose Canadians in favour of the free-
de agreement argued that access to the
ge American market would make it
sible for Canadian companies to grow
 contribute more to the Canadian
nomy. Those against the free-trade deal
 that the greatest effect of free trade
uld be the loss of jobs and industry to
 United States. According to that view,
nadian industry would not be able to
npete with much larger companies
th of the border.

e Liberals and New Democrats were
inst free trade with the United States,
 it became the central issue of the 1988
ction campaign. The Canadian public
cted a majority Conservative
vernment in 1988, and the free-trade
eement was put into effect shortly after.

v modern election campaigns become
focussed as the 1988 federal election.
wever, it is more difficult to say what
ues are decisive in an election. Often,
ction campaigns are run on the basis
the candidates' political record
personality.

ny people were concerned about the impact
 trade would have on Canadian businesses.

VEB LINK
read about the Canada-United States free
ade agreement, go to www.canadianeconomy.
.ca/English/economy/1989economic.html.

Resolving Political Differences **9**

# First Ministers Conferences

**W**hen governments in Canada face common problems, they often meet to discuss them. These meetings sometimes take the form of first ministers conferences, where leading politicians from the provinces and from the federal government meet to exchange views and find solutions.

Originally, the idea of first ministers conferences came about as a way for Canadians to resolve political difference over the future of **Confederation**. In th 1960s, some provinces began to want more power to control their own resou and economies. Many Canadians thoug that provincial governments should hav

Provincial governments are led by a premier.

re power and the federal government
uld have less. Others believed that
ada needed a stronger central
ernment to be successful in the
ld economy.

t ministers conferences are a way for
adians to meet and express their views
to resolve differences about the future
he country. The **Constitution** Act of
2 was worked out in a number of these
ferences, and there have been many
1 meetings since then on other
stitutional issues.

many successes of past first ministers
ferences have convinced people that
se conferences are worth having.
prime minister and the provincial
miers now meet on a regular basis
iscuss constitutional issues, the
nomy, and other matters of concern
Canadians.

Gordon Campbell was first elected premier of British Columbia in 2001.
Campbell and other premiers meet at first ministers conferences to discuss
issues of importance to the people they represent.

re Trudeau was instrumental in negotiating
terms of the Constitution Act of 1982.

## Think About It

Federal–provincial First Ministers' meetings often involve much
negotiation, and sometimes these meetings help politicians reach
a consensus on future action. Why might there be difficulty
in reaching an agreement among provinces on political,
economic, and social issues?

# Clyde Wells

**C**lyde Wells was premier of Newfoundland and Labrador from 1989 to 1996. These were important ye: in federal–provincial relations due to efforts to pass the Meech Lake Accord. Clyde Wells played a pivotal role in the accord's negotiations, and his name wi always be closely tied to its downfall.

The Meech Lake Accord was designed t bring Quebec into the Constitution. In 1992, Canada's Constitution had been **repatriated** under the Constitution Act All of the provinces had signed the act except for Manitoba and Quebec. While Manitoba eventually accepted the act, Quebec did not, citing that the act did recognize Quebec's rights as a French-speaking society. The province's government agreed to accept the Constitution only if certain conditions were met. These conditions included acknowledging Quebec as a distinct society, expanding Quebec's constitutio veto, and giving Quebec a stronger say **Supreme Court of Canada** appointmer The Meech Lake Accord was created to meet these conditions.

While most of the provincial governme were willing to accept these conditions, Clyde Wells was not. He began actively campaigning against the accord, stating that it would seriously damage Newfoundland's status in the federal government. He also had strong reservations against declaring Quebec a distinct society.

The Manitoba legislature did not approve the Meech Lake Accord.

first minister's conference was called 1990 to discuss the accord. Under mense pressure, Wells agreed to support accord, but only provided it could be ated before the province's citizens er via a **plebiscite** or within the ovincial **assembly**.

e other premiers agreed to this dition. However, the accord had a ming deadline. If the provinces did not s the accord before the deadline, its ms would be forfeited.

e day of the deadline was a dramatic ment in Canadian history. In

Manitoba, an Aboriginal politician named Elijah Harper refused to approve the province's passing of the accord on the grounds that it did not support the rights of Canada's Aboriginal community.

The delay in the Manitoba **legislature** led to a delay in Newfoundland. Clyde Wells refused to bring the accord to a vote in Newfoundland's assembly because he felt there was not enough time to properly debate the issues before the deadline. These two actions resulted in the failure of the accord.

**WEB LINK**
To learn more about the Meech Lake Accord, go to
www.histori.ca/peace/page.do?pageID=260.

Public hearings are one way commissions collect information.

# Commissions and Task Forces

**W**hile it is sometimes necessary for Canadians to use attention-getting action to make their voices heard, the Canadian government also has a number of ways it seeks the views of citizens. Sometimes, the government takes a question directly to the people. It wants to hear the views of not only the most vocal groups in society, but of a large number of

the people affected. Such studies can be at the federal or provincial level and are often in the form of royal commissions, **commissions of inquiry**, and task forces

These commissions seek opinions from many people: MPs, senators, civil servan volunteer organizations, and individuals They have the power to force people to b nesses and to look at secret or private cuments as part of their study. Often, nmissions visit towns and cities across country. They advertise when and ere they will hold public hearings. They ite interested individuals and groups to mit papers on the problems being died and suggest what policies the ernment should adopt.

y important matters are handled by al commissions, which are created der the Great Seal of Canada. The at Seal gives royal commissions the nbolic approval of the Queen. This ws their great importance. They ally have well-known experts as mbers of the commission.

vernments create commissions in order get the public's advice on important tters. In this way, the government uses nmissions to get the information it ds to form policies and make laws. It tests the waters, to see which laws or icies might be unpopular.

gestions made by the Royal mmission on the Status of Women in nada, for example, are now part of nada's laws and government policy. ginning in 1968, the Commission velled all over Canada and heard 468 efs from individuals and groups. Some the Commission's suggestions resulted new laws, such as those that make it gal for women to be paid less than n for the same work.

nmissions and task forces are a good y to get information on an issue, but y are very costly. The 1982 Royal mmission on Economic Union and velopment Prospects, for example, I a budget of $21.8 million and took ee years to complete.

Sometimes, commissions seek the opinions of specific groups of people, such as volunteer organizations or civil servants.

## Think About It

Royal commissions hear evidence from citizens and make suggestions for action. While these commissions can be costly and time consuming, they let citizens speak directly to political decision makers. On what kind of issues would you like to advise the government?

Canada's second referendum was on the issue of conscription during World War II.

# Citizens Speaking Directly to Government

Sometimes, it is not enough for governments to hear the views of only a few citizens. Some issues are so controversial that governments want to know what the majority of people want. Also, when citizens feel that governments are not being responsive to their needs, they can organize a vote to give the government a majority view.

When a government is unsure of what people think, it sometimes holds a plebiscite or referendum. A plebiscite is a vote designed to measure public opinion on an issue. Plebiscites give all citizens in a country, province, or municipality the chance to express their views on a course of action the government is considering. The results of plebiscites, however, are not binding. Governments do not have to follow the majority view, although sometimes they feel obligated to do so.

Similarly, a referendum allows citizens to express their views by voting, but the results of the vote are binding. The people may accept or reject a course of action suggested by the government, and the government is supposed to act in agreement with the vote.

spite the difference in their definitions, terms "plebiscite" and "referendum" often used to mean the same thing: act of submitting a question to the ing public as a measure of public nion on an issue. Most referendums l plebiscites ask controversial stions, and governments often the results of these votes to ke policy decisions.

Canada's history, there have been only ee national referendums. The first was 1898 on the question of **prohibition**. n though a majority of people voted in our of a law prohibiting the sale and of alcohol, the majority was so slight t the government did not pass the law. e second national referendum was in ·2 on the issue of **conscription**. The ernment wanted to find out if citizens eed with its proposal that people be illy required to join the armed services. e law was intended to get more Quebec zens into the services. Although iada's citizens voted 80 percent in our of conscription, the people of ebec voted about 70 percent against A conscription law was enacted before end of the war. A third national rendum was held in October 1992 onsider the Charlottetown Accord a renewed federal structure.

ne provinces and municipalities allow citizens to ask for a referendum any question they would like the ernment to act upon. Usually, group or individual that wants a rendum must get a certain number eople to sign a petition. This shows government that the question is ortant enough for a vote.

In 1995, Quebec residents were asked to vote in a referendum to decide if the province should separate from the rest of Canada. Canadians rallied in Montreal to try to convince Quebec to remain part of the country.

# Commons and Senate Committees

Another way that citizens have input in the decision making process is through the committees of the House of Commons and the Senate.

After a **bill** has been approved in second reading, it usually goes to a committee for further study. Commons committees are made up of MPs from all parties to study and debate legislation in detail. Part of the study includes hearing briefs from citizens representing either an interest group or their own views. The citizens' views are taken into consideration as part of the process for amending proposed legislation.

There are a number of committees that hear citizens' briefs, including Senate committees, which are composed of senators, usually with a particular interest or knowledge of the issue being addressed. There are also **joint committees**, made up of both members of **parliament** (MPs) and senators; and standing committees, which study problems on an on-going basis.

All these committees let citizens speak directly to those who make the laws. In many cases, the experience and insight of private citizens has had great effect on legislation as it passes through the committee system.

# Citizens Make Decisions: Linking Prince Edward Island

It would be too time-consuming and costly for governments to go directly to the citizens every time a decision must be made. For this reason, citizens elect people to express their views in government. However, governments can still become confused about how citizens feel about an issue. When this happens, a referendum or plebiscite may be the answer.

This was the approach Prince Edward Island's government took when considering the construction of a bridge linking the island to New Brunswick. This bridge, now known as Confederation Bridge, was built as a result of a provincial plebiscite.

For more than a century, the people of Prince Edward Island had debated whether or not to build a bridge or tunnel linking their island to the mainland. Some islanders felt that such a project would create jobs, boost tourism, and open up new markets for business people in P.E.I. Others argued a bridge would harm fishing in the area, threaten the environment, and eliminate jobs for those who ran ferries to and from the mainland.

The federal and provincial governments had been considering options for linking the island to the mainland for years. In the 1960s, for example, the federal government mapped out a plan for a bridge and tunnel between P.E.I. and New Brunswick, but the proposal was criticized as being too costly. As well, many were concerned about how it would affect shipping in the area. As a result, the federal government did not pursue the plan.

The debate continued, and finally the province's government decided to ask the islanders how they felt. A plebiscite on the issue was held in January 1988. The government asked the people of P.E.I. whether they wanted to join their province to New Brunswick with a link such as a bridge or tunnel. Of the people who voted, 59 percent favoured a link.

The results of the plebiscite encouraged both the provincial and the federal government to move ahead with the bridge. Construction started in 1992.

Confederation Bridge was completed in 1997, at a cost of about $1 billion.

**WEB LINK**
For more information on Confederation Bridge, go to www.confederationbridge.com.

# Case Study: The Special Joint Committee on a Renewed Canada

In early 1991, the country's constitutional talks were stalled. Quebec had resumed debate about separating from Canada, and many citizens were concerned that the government was not seeking their views on a new Constitution. Many citizens wanted to speak directly to government, especially after the Meech Lake Accord had been drafted in 1987 with no public input. When talks about Canada's Constitution began again in 1991, the federal government went directly to the people.

One joint committee that called for direct input from thousands of Canadians was the federal Parliament's Special Joint Committee on a Renewed Canada. The committee was formed in 1991 after the Meech Lake Accord had failed to bring Quebec into the Constitution a year earlier. The joint committee was given six months to "inquire into and make recommendations to Parliament on the Government of Canada's proposals for a renewed Canada." In simpler terms, the committee was asked to help develop a plan that would bring all of the provinces and territories into the Constitution.

Twenty members of the House of Commons and ten members of the Senate made up the committee, which was known as the Beaudoin-Dobbie committee after its chairpersons, Senator Gerald Beaudoin and Manitoba MP Dorothy Dobbie. The committee was instructed to give all Canadians, including special groups such as Aboriginal People, a chance to help create the new constitutional proposal. Its members were allowed to travel throughout the country, hold public hearings, meet with members of various legislatures, question experts on certain issues, and grant media coverage of the committee's activities.

The Beaudoin-Dobbie committee drew much public interest and media attention during its six months of discussions and meetings. Between the committee's first public meeting on September 21, 1991 and the submission of its report on February 28, 1992, the 30 members visited every province and territory and attended five national constitutional conferences in cities across Canada. A total of 3,000 written statements were received by the committee, and 78 public meetings were held. The meetings amounted to 227 hours of hearings, with statements from 700 Canadians.

As part of the Meech Lake Accord, Quebec wanted special recognition as a distinct society.

ter travelling the
untry and listening to
nadians, the committee
 to work on a 130-page
ort for Parliament. The
ort focussed on two
es of challenges the
untry faced: inclusion
d vision. The challenge
inclusion referred to
 need for Quebec, the
st, Atlantic Canada,
original Peoples,
men, and people from
cultures to feel included
Canada. The challenge
vision referred to the
untry's need for clear
itical, social, and
nomic goals. Vision also meant
eloping a way to reach those goals.

The Beaudoin-Dobbie committee report stated that Supreme Court judges be selected from a list provided by the provinces and territories.

e committee presented its report
Parliament as a starting point for
stitutional talks between Ottawa
 the provinces. It said as many
ernments as possible should be
olved in the discussions and these
s should begin as soon as possible.
 report suggested that Canada's
nstitution include a **preamble** and that
 "Canada clause" should clearly state
 country's values. It said Quebec
uld be recognized as a distinct society,
ere "distinct" refers to a unique culture,
rench-speaking majority, and a system
ivil law. It also suggested that
original Peoples receive the right to
-government, and that their consent
ought on all constitutional debates
t affect them. It said senators should
lected, and Supreme Court of Canada
ges should be chosen from a list of
didates submitted by the provinces
 territories.

The committee members felt their talks
with Canadian citizens were critical to
the proposal they finally made. In fact, in
the report's conclusion, the committee
wrote: "We believe the process of public
consultation and public involvement in
the constitutional process should continue
in various forms across the country.
Canadians have much to offer the
constitutional process and mechanisms
should be established to allow them to
make their views known."

## Think About It

What issues might people from your province have raised at the committee's hearings?

# Active Citizenship: Religious Freedom in Canadian Schools

**Gurbaj Singh won the right to wear a kirpan to school.**

When individuals have the courage and determination to challenge a decision or law, sweeping changes can result. Such was the case when the Multani family decided to fight for their son's right to wear his kirpan to school.

One day, while playing in the schoolyard at his school in Montreal, twelve-year-old Gurbaj Singh Multani accidently dropped his kirpan. A kirpan is a ceremonial dagger that baptized Sikhs are required to wear. To Sikhs, the kirpan is a symbol of their religion. School authorities, however, thought otherwise and viewed the kirpan as a potential weapon.

The school's principal demanded that Gurbaj Singh remove the kirpan. As this is against the principles of his religion, Gurbaj Singh refused the demand and was ordered to leave the school.

Gurbaj Singh remained out of school for several weeks while his parents negotiated with the school board to ensure that their son could wear his kirpan. Eventually, both parties came to an agreement. Gurbaj Singh could wear the kirpan at school as long as it was in a sheath that had a sewn flap. This ensured that the kirpan could neither fall out nor be taken out deliberately.

The problem seemed to be solved, but when Gurbaj Singh went back to school, he was once again sent home. This time it was because other parents were concerned about having the kirpan in the school. The issue went back to the school board, and it overturned its previous decision. Gurbaj Singh was again not allowed to wear his kirpan.

Carrying a kirpan is just one of many Sikh traditions. Sikhs also do not cut their hair. Males wear a turban over their long hair.

In response to this decision, the Multani's asked their lawyer to launch an appeal with Quebec's Superior Court. The Superior Court ruled in favour of the Multani's on the grounds of religious freedom. The court set conditions similar to those the school originally set. As long as the kirpan was securely attached to Gurbaj Singh's body, he could return to school wearing it.

The school board appealed the Superior Court's decision, and the Quebec Court of Appeal overturned the court's decision, saying that public safety was more important than religious freedom. In response, the Multani's lawyer launched another appeal, this time to the Supreme Court of Canada.

The decision of the Supreme Court was unanimous. All of the judges agreed that banning kirpans from schools violated Canada's **Charter of Rights and Freedoms**. Gurbaj Singh, now 17 years old, was finally given absolute permission to wear his kirpan to school.

## Think About It

Can you think of any situation in which public safety should take precedence over religious freedom?

# Building Citizenship Skills:
# Gaining Perspective

In order to effectively resolve issues, political or otherwise, it is important that all viewpoints on the issue are understood and valued. What one person or group feels about the issue may be very different from what other people feel. However, that one person may have valid reasons for feeling the way he or she does.

Obtaining a driver's license is a key moment in the lives of most Canadians. Yet, debate often occurs over how old someone should be before getting behind the wheel of a car. The following statements illustrate the differing opinions people have on this subject.

1) Which opinion do you agree with the most? Which do you relate to the least?

2) How do you think these opinions would compare to those of the insurance industry, driving instructors, or paramedics?
3) What do you think they would recommend for a legal driving age? Why would they recommend this?
4) What facts could be supplied to argue for or against their opinions?

### Interest Group #1: Students

By the time people enter high school, th are ready to drive an automobile. Stude are more mature than they used to be, a they need a car to be able to meet with friends and attend social events. At the a of 13 and 14, students are often asked to look after young children as babysitters, and many make extra money doing this students are responsible enough to care

small children, surely they are
ponsible enough to drive a car. It
he right of people to drive cars, and
ong as they are physically able, age
uld not be a problem.

## erest Group #2: Parents
teen is young enough for a legal driving
. Students 14 or 15 years old are not
ponsible enough, and even if some are,
just too early to have kids driving these
tly machines. We parents usually buy
cars, pay the registration and
urance fees, and pay for gas and repairs,
we should be making the final decision.
e could be sure that students would
ays use the vehicles in a responsible
nner, it might be different, but we're
not prepared to wave goodbye to our
s and our cars for the sake of a year or
of driving freedom.

## Interest Group #3: Police
I have seen more accidents involving
young drivers than any other kind. It is
always the same: students go out on a
weekend, get excited, race their cars, and
bang, four of them are dead or injured.
This happens with many young drivers
because they do not have the experience
behind the wheel to avoid accidents. Nor
do they have the experience with accidents
and death to know how ugly they really
are. The driving age should be raised to 18,
and that would save many lives, a great
deal of heartbreak, and millions of tax
dollars spent on police time, accident
clean-up, insurance payments, and
hospital care.

## What Can You Do?
Research facts to support your opinion on this subject.
Use this information to write a letter to your local
government representative that outlines the steps you feel
the government should take in deciding the legal driving age.

# What is Your Viewpoint?

**H**ow effective are Canadian citizens in reaching decisions? Canadians sometimes fee[l] that their voices are not heard by those who make important decisions. Each of these fictional Canadians feels differently about the way our system works.

### Viewpoint #1

Even though our system is a **democracy**, I do not feel my voice is really heard. Sometimes, it seems that citizens' opinions are reflected in the political process, but at other times, I feel frustrated. It seems that those in power work independently, neglecting their duty to represent their constituents. Or they act too slowly, dragging their heels because they want to play everything safe. Of course, the great thing about democracy is that you can get rid of ineffective or irresponsible politicians when their term is up. A politician's performance is measured in every election. That is one time when the people's voices get heard.

### Viewpoint #2

Democracy is an orderly and effective way of solving society's problems. Whe[n] you think of 26 million people from so many different cultures, it is amazing th[at] country has lasted this long. We have a system that lets people talk and work together on a wide range of issues. Anyc[ne] can participate and have a sense that the[ir] input counts. Canada works because citizens can communicate and participa[te.] Government leaders hear what we say and can respond to our needs.

### :wpoint #3

)vernments have to listen to the people,
d too often, they do not. This creates
strust among a country's citizens. Why
you think we have had a minority
vernment for so long? This is because
nada's citizens do not believe the
vernment is acting on their behalf. They
: unwilling to give the government a
jority because they do not trust that the
vernment will do what the people want.
he people felt any of today's political
rties was acting in the best interests of
nadians, they would vote that party in
h a majority. Right now, the people do
t feel they are being listened to.

### Viewpoint #4

I think elections are pretty reliable in
involving everyone in our political
decision making. Political decision
making begins at election time. Individual
Canadians get to say who should be in
government. The way our system works,
the candidate who gets the most votes
wins. In some cases, though, having the
most votes does not necessarily mean
that a majority of the voters in that
**constituency** voted for or wanted that
candidate. However, it is as fair a system
as we can get. It is a way of putting
responsible people in charge of a
country. If they do not perform well
while in office, they will not make it
through another election.

# Take the Citizenship Challenge

1. Get together with some friends, and try to come to a consensus on each of these four questions. Limit discussion on each topic to seven minutes.

   a) Where could the group meet for lunch together?
   b) What car is best for a first-time owner?
   c) Would lowering unemployment benefits decrease unemployment?
   d) What should the minimum penalty be for a first-time shoplifter?

   Were you able to come to an agreement on any of the topics? If a compromise was reached, how well did it satisfy all members? What are some of the reasons it is difficult for a group of individuals to agree on an issue?

2. With your friends and family, discuss the advantages and disadvantages of laws that require people to use safety equipment, such as seat belts, bicycle or motorcycle helmets, and smoke detectors. What are the objections people have to these laws? Why do legislators think that having these laws is a good idea?

3. Write a brief report expressing your own viewpoint about one of the following issues:

   a) Seat-belt legislation
   b) Voting-age legislation
   c) Environmental-protection legislation
   d) Freedom of speech

   Explain the reasons why you hold this viewpoint, and back it up with as many facts as you can. Read your report to your friends or family. Ask for their viewpoints on the issue. How different are their viewpoints from yours? What are the different facts that back up opposing viewpoints? Thinking objectively, are all viewpoints valid?

4. Write a short review about a movie you have seen or a book you have read about a person in conflict with "the system." Describe the reasons for the person's rebellion, the means the person uses to change things, and evaluate whether the struggle was successful or worth the cost.

**Q** What is the main purpose of an election?

**A** Elections are held to decid which candidates will best represent the citizens' interest and which group of candidates will form the government.

**Q** Why are the first ministers conferences held?

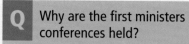

**A** The first ministers conferences are seen as a way for Canadians to resolve political differences over the future of Confederation.

**Q** Name two ways that the government gets advice directly from citizens on issues facing the country.

**A** The government uses commissions and task forces when it wants the advice of its citizens.

**Q** How can citizens express their concerns about the laws and policies a government tries to pass?

**A** Citizens can express their concerns to the government by appearing before Commons and Senate committees.

**Q** What is a referendum?

**A** A referendum is the submission of a question to the voting public as a measure of public opinion on an issue. The results of a referendum are normally binding.

**Q** How many national referendums has Canada held? What were the issues presented in the vote?

**A** Canada has had three national referendums. The first one asked the public to vote on prohibition. The second asked citizens to vote on conscription. The third referendum concerned the acceptance of the Charlottetown Accord as a renewed federal structure.

# Further Research

## Suggested Reading

Coyne, Deborah. *Roll of the Dice: Working with Clyde Wells during the Meech Lake Negotiations.* Toronto, Ontario: Lorimer, 1992.

Johnston, Richard. *The Challenge of Direct Democracy: The 1992 Canadian Referendum.* Montreal, Quebec: McGill-Queen's University Press, 1996.

Simeon, Richard. *Federal-Provincial Relations: The Making of Recent Policy in Canada.* Toronto, Ontario: University of Toronto Press, 2006.

## Internet Resources

To see what kinds of issues royal commissions have examined since Confederation, go to **www.collectionscanada.gc.ca/indexcommissions/index-e.html**.

Read the details of the Constitution Act of 1982, which includes Canada's Charter of Rights and Freedoms, at **http://laws.justice.gc.ca/en/const/annex_e.html**.

Learn more about House and Senate Committees at **http://canadaonline.about.com/od/senatecommittees/Senate_Committees_in_Canada.htm**.

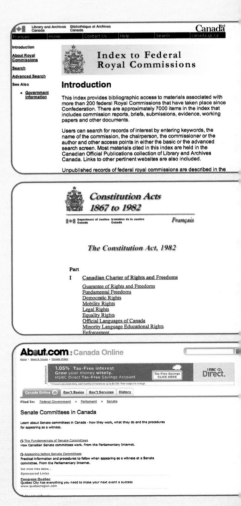

# lossary

**...embly:** a legislative body made ...p of people who were elected ...o represent an area's citizens

**...l:** a proposed law brought ...efore a provincial legislature or ...arliament for reading, debate, ...tudy, and possible approval

**...arter of Rights and Freedoms:** ...he part of Canada's ...Constitution that describes ...he political and civil rights ...f all Canadians

**...il law:** a system of law based ...olely on written documents

**...mmission of inquiry:** a group ...f people appointed by the ...overnment to investigate ...certain situation, gather ...nformation, and submit ...report of its findings to ...he government

**...nfederation:** the political ...nion of Canada's provinces ...nd territories

**...scription:** the act or system ...f forcing people to join the ...rmed forces

**constituency:** a specified area where voters elect a representative

**constitution:** a document detailing the fundamental principles on which a country is governed

**democracy:** a political system, sometimes called rule by the people, in which the people elect their government

**free trade:** international business between two or more countries that has no political interference, specifically in the form of tariffs, or taxes

**joint committee:** a group of members of Parliament and senators appointed to study certain issues with direct input from citizens

**legislature:** a body of persons vested with power to make and repeal laws

**liable:** legally responsible

**parliament:** the national law-making body of a democratic country, which in Canada includes the monarch, the elected House of Commons, and the appointed Senate

**plebiscite:** a public vote that is not binding on the government but intended to measure public opinion on an issue

**preamble:** an introductory or preparatory statement

**prohibition:** the time in history when it was against the law to make, buy, or drink alcoholic liquors in any form

**repatriated:** sent back to the country of origin

**Supreme Court of Canada:** the highest appeal court in Canada, having nine judges and dealing with civil and criminal matters

# Index